Gainsborough Old Hall

A guide to Gainsborough Old Hall
by Sue Allan

Almost hidden away in the north-west corner of Lincolnshire,
magnificent Gainsborough Old Hall is one of the most impressive
and best-preserved medieval manor houses in England.

Built by the noble Burghs, the Old Hall has been owned,
as well as lived in, by just one other family,
the Hickmans who arrived in Gainsborough in 1596.

With muted reds of warm Tudor brickwork set against
romantic black and white timber framing, this grand old lady of Gainsborough
has stood watch over the town and River Trent for more than five centuries.

Architectural features

For the greater part, the construction of Gainsborough Old Hall is of timber-framing as can most readily be seen within the interior (and exterior) of the Great Hall, one of the oldest parts of this building.

Hickman-Bacon family crest

The English oak for this was almost certainly sourced locally from the great swathe of forest that once formed a part of the surrounding Old Hall estate. Trees with a natural curve in their growth would have been especially sought after in order to construct the great arched roof beams. Samples taken from these in the Great Hall suggest that these oaks were felled somewhere around 1460. The fact that ugly cross braces were not used to support the impressive timber arches, has endowed the Great Hall with a serene and almost church-like feeling.

The spaces between the timber uprights used to build the walls were in-filled horizontally with pieces of wood called 'laths'. In turn these were then covered over with 'plaster' consisting of a mixture of such things as dust, horse hair, lime, lime-ash and animal dung in several coats of decreasing coarseness. At the time this was a very common form of building construction:

"The greatest part of our building in the cities and good towns of England consisteth only of timber, for as yet few of the houses of the communalty (except here and there in the west country towns) are made of stone....'these english", quoth he (a Spaniard of Queen Mary's day), *"have their houses made of sticks and dirt, but they fare commonly so well as the king."*

William Harrison, Description of England, 1587

GROUND FLOOR PLAN

The floor of the Great Hall would have originally comprised of compressed earth which was probably then consolidated by the addition of a layer of fresh ox blood. The floor tiles in situ today are a later addition.

Looking towards the end of the hall there are three doorways: the centre one leads to the kitchen flanked by the buttery and pantry to the right and left. Originally these functionary rooms would have been partially shielded from the view of the Lord's table by a huge screen that once spanned the far end of the hall. There might also have once been a minstrel gallery above. Although the screen has long since been removed, marks can still be seen in the timbers where it was once attached. Below is an impression of how the screen might once have looked.

Heating for the Great Hall was by means of a central fire. Set into the roof above there was once a 'louvre' to draw smoke and fumes upwards and out of the building. (The framework of the original louvre turret is now upstairs next to the tower bedroom). The louvre also let in additional light. The Lord and his table would have enjoyed extra heating by means of portable braziers.

The bay window of dressed stone or 'ashlar' does not appear to have been especially designed for the Great Hall. It is of late perpendicular-style with fine two light tracery of such high quality that suspicion arises that it must have been looted from a dissolved religious house after Henry VIII's break with Rome. Because the vault is clearly late Elizabethan or Jacobean, it has been suggested that it was therefore inserted at that time.

Stained glass panel

However, equally plausible is that the structure was originally incorporated into the hall much earlier during the 1500's but then needed repair later. In any case, the inclusion of this window was intended as a sign of wealth and to cast extra light upon the high status end of the hall.

In early photographs two stained-glass panels can be seen still in place in the bay window. During the 1960's, one bearing the royal coat of arms, was removed and framed, albeit inside out.

Originally the other windows, set high on each side of the Great Hall, would not have been glazed. Glass was a highly expensive commodity in the C15th and when used, if the Lord of the Manor travelled away from Gainsborough for any length of time, it would have been removed and taken with him. Instead of glass, linen coated with a mixture of sheep fat and wax could be used instead for windows. In bad weather this could be supplemented with wooden window shutters or hides to keep back the wind and the rain, however with the consequent loss of much natural light.

The Function of a Great Hall

The notion of a great hall, a large principal room in aristocratic domestic buildings has existed from pre-Saxon times and on into the Tudor/Jacobean era. Over time this developed from being an independent building into instead, as at Gainsborough Old Hall, the heart of a large house. It would have served also as the hub of the estate with people constantly coming and going. At Gainsborough Old Hall, the Great Hall with its kitchen would have been built first.

In early times, ordinary folk attached to the wider household depended entirely upon the Lord of the Manor for their every day existence, often working for their 'keep' rather than for pay. As a result, it was usual for household members to come inside their particular great hall at the end of the day. On locking the hall doors for the night – the ceremony of 'All-night' – the household would then settle down to sleep communally. For medieval people, darkness and the night were a fearful time when trouble, robbers, or danger lurked, or when even ghosts or evil spirits might be abroad! It was this idea of there being safety in numbers that bore overriding consideration, far above any idea of 'personal privacy'. In fact at this time the concept of a bedroom as we know it today was unknown.

Amid this communality, there would have been a strict social pecking order understood by all, as to where one could and could not go within the Great Hall itself. There would have been a 'lower end' to the hall (with services attached such as the kitchen) and the socially lower order of the household would remain in that part.

Then there was an 'upper end' to the hall, the focal point of which would have been the Lord's high table set upon a dais and beneath a large canopy. This area was only for those 'closest' to the Lord and it was at this end were the Lord's accommodations were (such as the private withdrawing area known as 'The Parlour'). Set beside the dais would be the Lord's 'buffet' – a sort of cupboard – on which the family plate of either silver or gold would have been displayed as a sign of his great wealth, again not a place for the lowly to be found straying.

Great Hall roof and colourful heraldic banners

The floors of the Great Hall would have been strewn with rushes – or 'thresh', which soaked up spillages and made the environment more comfortable. It was also very practical as it was easy for soiled thresh to be gathered up and replaced with new.

Beds for the lower orders of the household consisted of a sack or 'tick' woven from hemp that would then be filled with hay (hence the saying 'hitting the hay' for going to bed). Moreover, ordinary medieval people often slept with their heads on a log for support.

The great central fire (along with others in the rest of the house) had to, by law, be put out at night at around eight o'clock. The Law 'couvre feu'was designed to help protect buildings from accidently burning down at night as people slept. This led to our modern word 'curfew'. However, once the flames were out a large earthenware cover (also called a couvre feu) could be placed over the hot embers thus safely keeping the heat going for long after.

The other main function of a great hall was as a place for the household to take its main meals.

However, once the West Range at Thomas Burgh II's newly completed manor house was built, Gainsborough Old Hall would have run upon much more sophisticated lines. At 'All-night' only sworn members of the Lord of the Manor's staff, family or special guests would have been allowed to remain inside the Manor House, and mostly these occupied the West Range.

By the late 1400's, in keeping with the practice of other noble families, Lord Burgh and his family would have by far preferred to have kept themselves as distant from their common servants as possible and undoubtedly remained within their luxurious private apartments much of the time.

The Great Hall is where banquets would have been held. Imagine the Great Hall; a riot of colour with brightly decorated flags hung from the roof and with everyone dressed in their finest clothes. Minstrels would have no doubt made merry music as course after course of the finest foods were introduced to the diners accompanied by the fanfare of a trumpet.

Status would dictate each person's place at these meals. Therefore the higher your status then the nearer to the Lord's table you were seated. The nearer to the Lord that you sat, the higher was the quality of the meal you received. Even what your meal was eaten from depended upon your social standing and therefore might range from a slice of stale bread to a wooden trencher or onwards up to plates made of pewter, silver or even gold.

Table etiquette of the late 15th and 16th centuries was also surprisingly strict and fellow diners would scorn any breach made. Although knives and spoons were used for most courses, for taking food from communal dishes fingers sufficed, hence an important part of good manners was to be seen washing one's hands before helping oneself to such food. Thus dishes of water scented with herbs or flower petals water accompanied by towels were proffered to diners at intervals throughout the meal.

Visitors of Note

On October 10th, 1483, King Richard III stayed the night at Gainsborough Old Hall on his way to London from York. However, shortly after this his host, Thomas Burgh II, appears to have switched his allegiance to the King's Lancastrian opponent, Henry Tudor, and soon Richard would be dead.

In August 1541, King Henry VIII visited Gainsborough Old Hall on his way from Lincoln to York. 'Letters and Papers, Foreign and Domestic, Henry VIII 1541' show that the King left Lincoln on the Friday (12th) for Gainsborough and meetings of the Privy Council are recorded as having taken place at Gainsborough on the 14th, 15th and 16th – showing that Henry stayed at the Old Hall for three days.

It is not clear if Henry and Queen Catherine Howard actually slept at the Old Hall during those nights or not. At Lincoln it is recorded that: 'The King and Queen came riding into their tent, which was pitched at the furthest end of the liberty of Lincoln, and there shifted their apparel, from green and crimson velvet respectively, to cloth of gold and silver...' However, after a service at the Cathedral it was then also noted 'Then all went straight to their lodgings for the night...' suggesting that the royal party probably did not sleep in their tents but indoors elsewhere.

If Henry and Catherine slept within the Old Hall, then several chambers might well have been deemed suitably fine enough to accommodate them. However, contrary to popular belief the king is unlikely to have used the upper bedchamber in the tower. By this time Henry was very obese and his long-standing problem of painful, ulcerated legs would have made it extremely difficult to climb the narrow staircase.

Great Hall bay window

Later history of the Great Hall

By the end of the Tudor era, the Old Hall no longer paid host to royal visitors. By William Hickman's time, the Great Hall had become little more than a yawning, little-used space with his lordship quietly dining elsewhere.

Yet this was by no means to mark the end of the Great Hall's usefulness. John Smyth's Gainsborough congregation of Separatists may have gathered in this place for their meetings while it is known that John Wesley certainly once preached here.

Even after the Hickman family had abandoned the Old Hall as its family residence in the 1700's in favour of a new hall at Thonock, the Great Hall continued to be used as a public venue, a fact that no doubt led to its ultimate survival into modern times.

At first, the Great Hall served as the town's public hall. Then in 1790 Mr. West, an entrepreneur, leased the Great Hall and fitted it out as a theatre, complete with seats and a gallery.

When the then owner Lady Frances Hickman died her successor, Henry Bacon Hickman, wanted to refurbish the Great Hall and turn it into the Corn Exchange. However the theatre continued on for many years until in 1849 it was reported; 'the theatre... has been demolished, the large banqueting hall in which the theatre was fitted up, is to be restored'.

By this time the Old Hall in general was in a very poor state and so railway engineer, Denzil Ibbetson, was engaged to undertake repairs. Ibbetson was responsible for the cast iron corbels that can still be seen today at the lower ends of the arched roof braces in the Great Hall. It was also about this time that the Great Hall's north door was replaced with a window and the woodcarvings made.

Burgh Family Time Line
Thomas Burgh I
Died 1432

Thomas Burgh II
1432-1496
Built Gainsborough Old Hall

Edward Burgh
c1464 –1528

Thomas Burgh III
C 1488-1550
Chamberlain to Queen Ann Boleyn

William Burgh
1522-1584

Thomas Burgh IV
c1558-1597
Sold Gainsborough Old Hall

Hickman Family Time Line
Lady Rose Hickman
1526-1613

William Hickman
1549-1625
Bought the Old Hall 1596

Willoughby Hickman
1604-1649

William Hickman
1628-1682

Willoughby Hickman
1659-1720

Neville Hickman
1701-1733
Built new hall at Thonock

Neville George Hickman
1725-1781

Lady Frances Hickman
1747-1826
On death the Old Hall passed into Bacon family

Henry Bacon Hickman
1788-1862

Sir Henry Hickman Bacon
1820-1872

Sir Hickman Beckett Bacon
1855-1945

Sir Edmund Castell Bacon
1903-1982

Sir Nicholas Hickman Ponsonby Bacon
b1953-
President of the Friends of the Old Hall Association

These two service rooms are situated either side of the central passage leading towards the kitchen.

Pantry comes from the French word for bread, 'pain' which indeed would be amongst other items of cold, cooked food temporarily stored in this area prior to use in the Great Hall. Expensive table linen and other pieces of tableware were also stored here. Overseeing the Pantry was the 'Pantler'

Buttery comes from the French word for bottle – 'bouteille'. However in medieval times most beverages like ale, mead were stored in barrels – or 'butts' – which were brought up from the cellar and into the buttery to settle before then being transferred into jugs prior to serving at table. Wine was usually stored in a separate cellar.

The man in charge of the Buttery was called a 'butler' and he was responsible for not only the drinks but also the drinking vessels. Both the Pantler and the Butler would answer to the Steward of the house and both rooms would be kept under lock and key.

GROUND FLOOR PLAN

Evidence in the form of trefoil-headed moulded bricks on the southern face of the passageway connecting the buttery and pantry to the kitchen suggest that this area may have originally been open, providing a fire-break between the Kitchen and the timber–framed Great Hall beyond. However as the Old Hall evolved this soon became built over forming the room above.

At the servery, food was collected from the two huge hatchways to be taken into the Great Hall. Far from being the job of minions, the servers were high-born young men residing at the hall in order to complete their education-which included instruction in social skills such as horsemanship, fighting arts, music and of course dining etiquette. Similarly, Lord Burgh's sons would have spent time learning these same skills at some other great manor house. This 'exchange programme' was also useful for networking – especially as noble families would be mindful of finding suitable prospective spouses for their own daughters' arranged marriages.

In the west wall of the Servery is a large arch which supports a fireplace in the rooms above.

Interesting Facts

Due to the near famine conditions of the winter of 1816/17, the Old Hall kitchen became a soup kitchen and during the course of sixteen weeks over twenty-thousand meals were passed out to the hungry from the servery hatches. (1816 was the notorious 'year without a summer' when crops failed across huge swathes of the northern hemisphere. This was due to the large amounts of ash accumulated in the atmosphere after the eruption of Mount Tambala in Indonesia.

GROUND FLOOR PLAN

These two rooms have been identified as the 'Stewards Chambers' as in the days of the early Lord Burghs.

The Steward was the Lord of the Manor's most senior, trusted servant who shouldered the myriad day to day responsibilities related to the smooth running of Old Hall estate and beyond. The use of this space for this purpose would make perfect sense as both rooms are within handy reach of the West Range and Kitchen where many of the household servants worked and slept.

The first room, a parlour, is accessed directly by the staircase to the left of the servery hatches. It has a small chimney in the east wall and to the north there is a garderobe/latrine. It is here that the 'muniment' (documents proving ownership of property) and bullion (gold and silver) chests were probably located along with the counting tables. Each morning and afternoon, the Steward and the senior staff held a meeting to discuss business, food and menus as well as general running of the Manor. In the Royal household, and the Lords' private chambers at Parliament, such meetings were held around a table covered in green baize cloth and so known as meetings of the green cloth , and this practice may have been emulated by noble households, like the Burgh's.

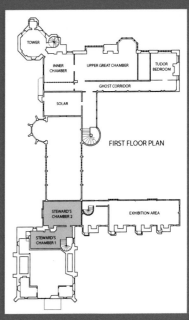

Amongst those attending these meetings would be the Steward, Cook and Kitchen Clerk, as well as representatives from other working departments attached to the Old Hall. Here clerks would deal with accounting, audit, letters, and all the other things needed to run His Lordship's business

The adjoining room is accessed from the first and is lit by a large window in the north wall. It also has a large fireplace. This room was almost certainly used by the Steward as his own private chamber. Here he likely housed his own office, complete with a bed and other luxuries befitting a highly regarded member of his Lordship's staff. Thomas Burgh II's Steward received the then princely salary of £25 per year.

These two rooms are probably the same ones listed as being the first and second 'Brighouse Chambers' in the William Hickman inventory of 1625. The first of these spans the area between the Great Hall and the Kitchen above the Servery just like a bridge or local word 'brig'. This also fits in with the fact that the Hickman family had owed and used ships for generations. The term 'bridge' was used on ships for the

command centre and so would equally be of fitting use here to describe the rooms allotted to their household Steward.

As the Great Hall (and therefore this second room housed in the cross-wing) was once separated from the kitchen, it has been suggested that this room might once have served as the Solar (although how it might have then been accessed is unclear).

Although the quite grand features of both rooms suggest an important function, this is somewhat undermined by the fact that the only apparent access is via the rather mean stairway more befitting servant status. Coupled with the close proximity to the lowly status kitchen with its noise and smell, it is unthinkable that any of Lord Burgh's immediate family would have chosen to occupy such a place.

This is undoubtedly one of the finest surviving domestic kitchens from the late medieval era. The body of the building, where the fire risk would have been greatest, is built of brick supplemented with timber framing where the risk was minimal. Brick was highly expensive at that time.

Although there is a similarity between the kitchen chimney stacks and those of the west range, with their polygonal brick-built pots, in comparison some of the original kitchen window openings are noticeably lacking in ornamentation - underlining the lowlier function of this building. Also absent from the kitchen is the elaborate moulding of the great hall timberwork, again hinting at its lesser status.

Strategically placed just inside the kitchen entrance is a small two-door room once used by the Clerk to the Kitchen. The Clerk was the man responsible for overseeing supplies of food etc. and managing the numerous kitchen staff and paying their wages. He also kept a watchful eye out for any pilfering. At a time when spices and then sugar were highly expensive, the Clerk also oversaw their careful distribution for use by the cooks, which incidentally at the time was a predominantly male profession.

Kitchen interior

GROUND FLOOR PLAN

On both the north and south walls are two gigantic fireplaces once used for cooking. Both are large enough to have taken an ox for roasting. However in the normal course of events, only the south fireplace would have been used for roasting meat and is equipped with a spit that a young boy would have been employed to turn.

The second fireplace would have been used for cooking such things as boiled meat, vegetables, or 'potage'. Potage was a hearty soup-cum-stew made up basically of what ever odds and ends came to hand in the kitchen, such as off cuts of meat, mixed with vegetables and barley. A warming bowl of pottage would have been very welcoming on a cold day, but one quite literally took 'pot luck' as to what your particular serving would contain.

Although there are purpose-built chimney stacks in the kitchen, up in the roof a louvre similar to that of the Great Hall helped clear the kitchen of excess smoke, steam and fumes and also to let in extra light. The louvre seen today is Victorian.

Built into the west wall is a twin oven, thought to be for pastry, although there has been speculation that there was once a separate bake house in the grounds of the Old Hall. There is not one listed on the 1625 inventory.

Whatever their purpose, all of this type of oven functioned in the same way. To heat the ovens brushwood tied into bundles or 'faggots' was either lit and pushed inside or was placed inside and then ignited by a smaller bundle of burning brushwood called a 'pimp'. The brushwood would have burned extremely quick and hot leaving the bricks inside heated to a high enough temperature for baking. As the brushwood naturally burned out, as much residue as could be quickly raked out was removed – but not too carefully as once the fire had died down the oven would immediately begin to lose precious heat. The uncooked pies or shaped bread dough would quickly be placed on the hot oven floor using a large paddle (often made of light poplar wood) called a 'peel'.

The oven opening would then either be plugged by a thick wooden door shaped to fit (which would have been made ready prior to use by soaking it in a pail of water) or with a

Kitchen exterior

metal plate, either of which could then have been sealed up using some excess bread dough to help keep the heat in. An experienced baker would have known instinctively when the contents were cooked and ready to come out and so then simply chipped away the cooked bread dough seal to open up the door.

Looking up inside the chimney by the ovens, bricks can be seen jutting outwards. These would have been used as foot and handholds for the boys regularly sent up to sweep them.

A corner room at the west end of the north wall (beside the ovens) is currently dressed as a preparation area for baked goods such as bread, with a storage space above for sacks of flour and a pulley system for moving them. In the opposite corner, there is another storeroom dressed as a game larder. Although there must have been such a store somewhere, it is unlikely in reality that it would have been placed here – next to the hot chimney breast. Instead this room may have contained a large copper for boiling water.

The 1625 Inventory mentions a scullery and two larders as being in the Kitchen as well as 'three chambers about the kitchen' which contained beds. Above the Kitchen there is also evidence of further structures, now lost, which may have once provided other places for more servants to sleep.

Both the East and West Range are believed to have been built in very quick succession after the Great Hall and Kitchen. Some wood samples seem to suggest that the West Range could be the slightly later building of the two.

Spread over three floors, this area which now has various modern uses was originally intended as a lodging block, complete with numerous garderobes and fire places (which were added after the original timber framed building had been completed). This building would have offered a high standard of comfort for the times.

In the 1625 Inventory, three chambers presumably in this range are assigned to named members of the household of that time – 'Mr. Dalderbig, James Potterton and Mr. Willoughby – (perhaps William Hickman's son and heir also named Willoughby).

During the Victorian era a part of the West Range was used as tenement housing and a pub.

Newel Staircase and Landing

The wide spiral staircase and the two storey annex that houses it was probably added at some stage during the Elizabethan era by the Burgh family. (Originally the Solar next to the landing would have to have been accessed by an earlier staircase, perhaps external, directly from the Great Hall's or adjoining Parlour beneath.)

Looking through the leaded lights, the raised beds below are a recent reconstruction of a garden from the medieval/Tudor period. They contain a sample of just some of the herbs and plants used at that time for healing and culinary purposes.

During William Hickman's time, there was a wall with a central gate connecting the two ranges and so enclosing the garden into a small courtyard with the Mart Yard beyond. In the Mart Yard – an enclosed outdoor area but in essence an extension of the Old Hall – a three day fair was held each year at Easter and in October.

Hidden from sight beyond the modern day houses to the west is the River Trent. Once the river ran much closer to the Old Hall and Gainsborough was a busy port exporting wool and other goods to Europe. The Lord of the Manor controlled this port and the river – crossing further along (where the bridge is today) from which a large part of the manorial income was generated.

Detail on West Range exterior

The Solar, situated in the cross wing above what was once the Great Hall's parlour, can best be described as a rather grand bed-sitting room rather than as an early bedchamber. It would be to this room that the Lord and his Lady, along with perhaps other family members and trusted 'intimate' servants could retire, away from the crowd and noise of the Great Hall.

The meaning of the word 'solar' is often described as being derived from the word 'solaris' – meaning the sun – as most solars are built facing south to make the most of the available natural light but not all are exclusively so. A more likely root for this word is from the French 'seul(e)' which means alone – referring to the privacy such a room might offer.

Most surviving solars from this time had a 'squint' window which allowed the Lord of the Manor to be able to look down upon the Great Hall to observe what those below were doing. As this part of the wall had been adapted in later years for use as a theatre, the original squint window would have been destroyed; therefore a replacement has been inserted in this solar in recent times.

The Solar, dressed with reproduction furniture of the period, provides a taste of what comforts there were to be enjoyed in the late C15th. Wicker fire screens protected noble ladies' delicate pale complexions, as did the reversible bench seat. Chests were used for storage and there is even an oak cupboard containing food and drink. Combined with the warm reed matting and the elaborate wall hangings this lends a rather cosy feeling to the room.

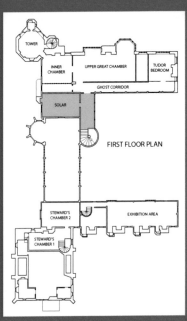

FIRST FLOOR PLAN

Unlike the three-storey West Range, when first built the East Range only had two floors. Instead of suites of rooms, here the larger ceremonial chambers were located. Although this part of the Old Hall was originally timber-framed, the ground floor of the west face was under built in brick during the 19th century. The south gable was encased by brick by William Hickman and according to antiquarian Adam Stark writing in 1813, was once adorned with a sundial dated 1600 and bearing the initials W.H and the inscription 'Deus mi – ut umbra sic vita' – 'My God, life is as a shadow'. Hickman also encased the east exterior with brick and inserted new stone- mullioned windows.

Radical changes were also made to the south end of this range by converting the existing two floors into three and then an additional staircase.

The Lord's private accommodation, which had previously centered upon the tower, was now relocated to the new lighter rooms, at the south end of the building which featured fine fire places. Meanwhile the house's main reception rooms remained located as they had been during the 15th century.

During the 1700's, after the Hickman family had moved to Thonock, the range became the grace and favour apartments of Lord Abingdon.

From 1896 until 1952, the Freemasons used two large rooms on the ground floor of the east range as their Lodge. A Mr. Edmund Dawber resided in the living accommodation at the south end of the range until his death in the 1970's.

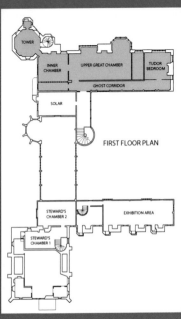

Corridor

Houses of this era were usually laid out as a series of linked rooms. The inclusion of a corridor is therefore an unexpected feature for its time.

For more than two centuries at least, reported sightings have been made of a ghostly apparition walking along the corridor towards the north end of the East Range. This female figure all dressed in grey, having reached the leaded lights then turns to disappear through a doorway leading towards the tower. As to whom she might be, many theories abound. Some say that she is a daughter of one of the Lord Burghs, who pined to death after having been forbidden to marry the man she loved. Others believe that she is the ghost of Queen Catherine Howard. If, while visiting the Old Hall you should see her, then please feel free to stop her and ask.

A ghost appears...

Inner Chamber

Once possibly the inner chamber of the Upper Great Chamber, this space now houses the large louvre turret that once sat on the Great Hall roof.

Looking at the outside wall, it is clear to see the original timber-framing now encased in late Tudor/Jacobean brickwork. In fact, with its exposed corridor timbers, this one of the best areas within the Old Hall to gain a clear understanding of how it was constructed and even adapted over time. However, if while visiting you are in any way uncomfortable about being inside a building of such a great age then it is perhaps best not to look up at the ceiling.

Louvre turret

Although it is difficult to determine the exact date that the polygonal tower was added to the East Range, it is quite likely that it was built around the mid 1480's. Maybe Thomas Burgh II having been elected as a Knight of the Garter under Richard III or perhaps his summons to the House of Lords in 1487 (after being created First Baron Gainsborough by Henry VII) would both have been occasions worthy of marking by such a fine addition to the family seat.

Although very military-looking in architecture, features such as the large widows on the top floor and the easy access to the lower rooms suggest that this tower's use was always intended as domestic rather than defensive.

The internal layout of the tower comprises three separate floors containing a single room with a fireplace and an adjoining garderobe, which are accessed by a spiral staircase of forty-five stone steps.

During the Burgh family's ownership, these rooms are thought to have formed a part of the lord's family apartments.

In the distant past it was possible to see much further from the top of the tower than today However, perhaps not as far as Adam Stark claims in his 'History of Gainsborough' written in 1813:

'The top of the tower commands a very extensive prospect of the whole of the course of the Trent, nearly to where it joins the Humber, the hills at Aukborough and Burton-Stather being easily seen; and from it the approach of any vessel is perfectly to be distinguished.'

The tower would have been very useful when looking out for ships on their way to Gainsborough – especially if they were gun-ships armed with cannon as during the English Civil War! Today there is a pleasant panorama of Gainsborough town, the parish church of All Saints and beyond.

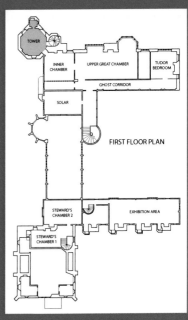

Interesting fact:

There are documentary hints that there may have once been two towers at Gainsborough Old Hall. After preaching in the grounds of the hall in June1786, John Wesley wrote: 'One of the towers is said to have been built in the reign of King Stephen, above six hundred years ago...'

Intriguingly William Burgh's will of 1496 also talks of a 'lowe towre': *"And also I will if my sonn Thomas life at the day of my buriell that he have... the bedde of the lowe towre and hanging and counterpoint of the said towre..."*

Why should Burgh have qualified his description with this adjective 'lowe' if there was only the one tower?

If there was indeed a second tower it does not appear on the 1625 Hickman inventory as being occupied – although the remains of a disused tower could have quite possibly been converted into a 'horse-mill' – of which there is one mentioned as being within the Old Hall grounds.

Adam Stark in his 'History of Gainsborough' does not mention a second tower. Instead he apparently ignores that possibility by quoting, quite scathingly, from a poem from The Lady's Museum, of October 1799:

> 'Mark where yon mould'ring edifice appears,
> The shatter'd remnant of devouring years;
> E'en now the towers a grandeur still display
> Which time itself can never take away.'

Where this 'missing' tower, if it existed, could have stood is a mystery, and likely to remain so as much of the Old Hall's once extensive grounds have since been built upon.

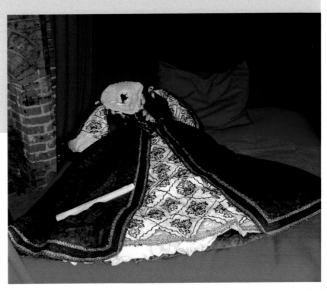

Upper Great Chamber

Throughout the C15th, C16th and on into the C17th, the Upper Great Chamber would have been used as the main ceremonial room on this floor by both the Burghs and the Hickmans. After the departure of the Hickman family to Thonock this room was still accorded high status.

During the C19th the wooden frame of the ceiling of the Upper Great Chamber was raised by about 75cm and the exterior brick-work built up accordingly. At that time the room was not divided as it is today and was used as the town's public assembly room.

The gothic-style fireplace, decorated with the Burgh family emblem- the 'Maynfer- or mailed fist and roses (suggesting the 'War of the Roses') was also added at this time. Two carved wooden panels above the doorways are of the same date.

Today one of the most notable things about this impressive space is the numerous portraits of past members of the Hickman and Bacon families.

Fireplace detail

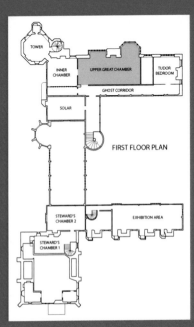

Created by William Hickman, this room could possibly be the one described as being his bed chamber in the 1625 inventory. The room today is dressed very much as it would have been in Sir William's lifetime.

The bed (although not the original) is very fitting owing to its intricate carvings depicting such biblical scenes as 'Cain killing Abel' and 'Adam and Eve in the Garden of Eden' as well as several beautiful angels. The head of the bed also has a secret compartment hidden amongst the carvings.

Above the bedroom (and now used as staff offices) is a suite of smaller rooms- almost certainly the 'nursery', and 'high chamber' also mentioned next in the inventory. The fact that there is a nursery may help to date closely these particular adaptations. Sir William's first wife Agnes had been childless during her previous marriage. Widowed and older, Agnes had remained childless during her second marriage and up until her death in February of 1600. William remarried almost immediately and soon needed a nursery to house his growing brood of young children

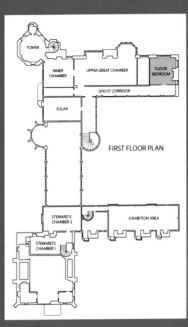

FIRST FLOOR PLAN

This room could possibly be the 'litle dineing parlor' of the 1625 inventory as the next item is described as 'the litle side parlor'. The creation of this room and the small one adjoing it are the result of the reordering of this end of the East Range during William Hickman's renovations. This is the only room to have retained its fine oak panelling.

According to Thomas Burgh II's will of 1496, this part of the range then contained a parlour, an inner parlour with an adjoining chamber. However 'reconstructing'the original layout of this ground floor area is difficult owing to the many changes it has undergone. Added to this, Hickmans rearrangement has also since been changed. Therefore, the original layout of much of the ground floor is uncertain.

In the small side chamber – now known as the Tyrwhitt Room – there is an intriguing piece of Tudor graffiti, thought to have been written during the 1541 visit by one of Henry VIII's courtiers. In the Hickmans' time this chamber may have served as a 'closet' where a close stool might have been kept – which is understandable considering the apparent lack of garderobes in this part of the building.

GROUND FLOOR PLAN

Gift and Tea Shop Area

At least a part of this ground floor area now serving as the Gift Shop (where the wall painting is) was listed as being the 'Garden Parlour' on the 1625 inventory. This would tie in nicely with both its position adjacent to the original Old Hall gardens and the apparent subject matter of the painting extending across both the plaster and beams of one wall. Stylistically this mural dates from the early 17th century. There is an earlier but much more extensive wall painting, similar in style and execution, at Ellys House, Great Ponton, near Grantham in Lincolnshire, which gives an idea of how exquisite the one at Gainsborough might once have been.

Gardens and exterior

No visit to Gainsborough Old Hall would be complete without stopping to stroll around the grounds and to take in the wonderful architectural features of the building's fascinating exterior.

On the east face wall of the East Range brickwork are four curious alcoves that never fail to intrigue visitors. These recesses are called 'bee boles' and each is just big enough to hold a hive made of coiled-straw or 'skep' as they are called. Beekeepers in England used these skeps before the introduction of modern-style wooden bee hives in the C19th.

Devoted volunteers of the Friends of Gainsborough Old Hall's gardening group lovingly tend the flowerbeds and parterre.

Wall painting at Ellys House, Great Ponton, near Grantham in Lincolnshire

Bee bole containing a skep

The Old Hall – a true survivor

Throughout her long existence, Gainsborough Old Hall has intermittently suffered from neglect, decay and near extinction. Yet through thoughtful and timely intervention, each occasion she has survived to come though such adversity stronger than before.

One such period of neglect, which had begun in the second half of the 1700s, led Thomas Miller to reminisce:

"It had been let off for a long time in separate rooms for shops and dwelling-places, to the great disgrace of the owner, for it was once one of the finest old baronial mansions that could be found within many miles... You peeped in and saw its great ground floor apartments occupied by joiners, and coopers, and bricklayers – depositories for their lime, hair and bricks – and you turned away in disgust.

In one of the few stained-glass windows that remained over the low broad archway, which commanded a view of the garden behind, and no doubt had, in former times, been beauty's bower, a mass of unsightly rags were stuffed through the centre of the deep-dyed shield."

On that occasion, it was Henry Bacon Hickman who came to the rescue and between 1847 and 1849 had engaged Ibbetson to carry out repairs and the restoration of the Great Hall.

Again, in 1878 repairs and renovations were undertaken, this time by the new owner, Henry's great-nephew, Hickman Beckett Bacon.

By the end of WWII, the Old Hall had fallen yet again into a state of dilapidation with the Great Hall, West Range and the north end of the East Range in serious danger of collapse.

It was at this time that a dedicated, forward-thinking group of local people, under the leadership of Harold Witty Brace, formed themselves into a voluntary organisation to carry out urgent repairs themselves to save the building. Thus 'The Friends of the Old Hall Association' came onto being with the noble aim of saving, preserving and promoting Gainsborough Old Hall so that it might carry on being enjoyed and appreciated by many future generations. The association is as active today as ever it was in its pursuits and always welcoming of new members.

Today, Lincolnshire County Council manages Gainsborough Old Hall while English Heritage owns it and cares for the fabric of the building. Much of the hall's furniture and paintings still belong to the Bacon family.

Events

At Gainsborough Old Hall history matters and so throughout the year colourful and exciting events are regularly held.

From Medieval re-enactors and crafts people 'inhabiting' the Old Hall, bringing alive a past way of life and filling the air with the cooking aromas of long-forgotten dishes to vintage car rallies, there is always something going on for all the family to enjoy. Added to this, are often a variety of talks and presentations hosted at the Old Hall throughout the year.

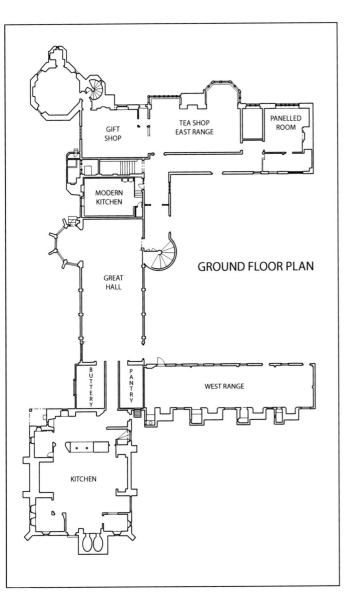

GROUND FLOOR PLAN

GIFT SHOP

TEA SHOP EAST RANGE

PANELLED ROOM

MODERN KITCHEN

GREAT HALL

BUTTERY

PANTRY

WEST RANGE

KITCHEN

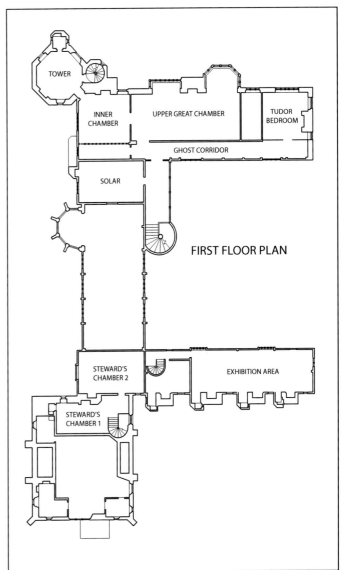

FIRST FLOOR PLAN

TOWER

INNER CHAMBER

UPPER GREAT CHAMBER

TUDOR BEDROOM

GHOST CORRIDOR

SOLAR

STEWARD'S CHAMBER 2

EXHIBITION AREA

STEWARD'S CHAMBER 1

Glossary

Corbel – a piece of stone, wood, or metal, often in the form of a bracket, projecting from the side of a wall and serving to support a cornice, the spring of an arch, etc.

Close stool – a commode or type of portable toilet.

Garderobe – is a medieval toilet emptying into a pit below. Soon it was discovered that fumes emanating up from the pit could be harnessed to kill off the lice and fleas that commonly inhabited ones clothing at this time. Garments, therefore, were routinely hung up in this toilet area for treatment thus giving it its name. The pits were regularly dug out and emptied by hand and the hapless people given that task were called gong farmers. Alternative names for the Garderobe were the privy, jakes, draught, and gong.

Tracery – ornamental work of interlacing or branching lines of stonework used to break up a larger space within a window or 'light'. As seen in the Great Hall bay window – each larger arched 'light' has been split into two parts.

Trefoil-headed – ornamental decoration or figure resembling a threefold leaf

Vault – an arched roof, ceiling, or covering of masonry.

Acknowledgements

Gainsborough Old Hall
Lincolnshire County Council
Lincoln Archives
FOHA
Roger Vorhauer
Brita Lakeman
Lord Burgh Retinue
Dr Philip Lindley
Rich Hines

The
Burgh
and
Hickman
Families

*The Burgh family origins appear to have been as farmers,
then becoming minor gentry, probably as wool merchants.*

Thomas Burgh II, Baron Gainsborough, 1432-1496

Thomas Burgh II was the only son of Thomas Burgh
Esquire, a survivor of Agincourt who had fought during the
'Hundred Years War' with France under Clarence the Bastard.
He died in December 1432, when Thomas II was just eight
months old and his mother pregnant with another child.

His mother, Elizabeth Percy, was a co-heiress to a junior
branch of the great Earls of Northumberland Percy family.
Amongst other lands, Thomas' mother Elizabeth had
inherited from her father a manor house at Gainsborough
with its fine estate. In turn, she had then left that estate to
her son upon her own death in 1455.

After enjoying a fairly quiet life, with the deposition of the
feeble King Henry VI and the accession of his young Yorkist
rival, Edward IV, thirty-year-old Thomas suddenly found
himself thrust into the heady mix of national affairs. Trusted
by the Yorkist lords, firstly in 1460 Thomas was named
Sheriff of Lincoln before then being entrusted to the position
of Esquire of the body of King Edward. Of these closest of
royal servants, The Black Book of regulations for the king's
household said 'theyre business is many secretes…'

Thomas Burgh II, Baron Gainsborough, 1432-1496

By Christmas 1462, Thomas had been created a knight and a
member of the Privy Council. The Burgh family star was
now truly in its ascendancy.

Some time between May 1462 and 1464, Thomas married
extremely well a rich noble widow Margaret, dowager Lady
Botreaux – daughter of the late Lord Thomas Ros – who
brought with her even more wealth and lands. However, it
is also possible that through this union Thomas Burgh's
new wife unwittingly endowed the Burgh family line with
the unwanted trait of madness.

At about this time, Sir Thomas began to build his manor
house at Gainsborough that we today fondly call the Old
Hall. This Hall would serve not only as a family home but
also as a demonstration of the Burghs' growing wealth and
importance.

However, with great success there often comes great envy. In
1470 when King Edward briefly lost control of the government
to the Earl of Warwick the hall was attacked by Thomas
Burgh's rival, Sir Robert Welles. Contemporary records report
that he 'pulled down his place, and took all of his goods and
chattels that they might find…' However, it is unclear exactly
how much damage the Old Hall sustained at that time.

After helping Yorkist King Edward IV escape from Middleham
Castle, Thomas Burgh joined him at the battle of Barnet on
the14th April 1471. After Edward's sudden death on 9th
April 1483, Burgh then turned his support to King Richard
III, during which time he was elected a knight of the garter.
However, soon after King Richard's visit to Gainsborough
Old Hall, Sir Thomas then switched his support to that of
Lancastrian Henry Tudor, Earl of Richmond instead. After the
death of King Richard and Henry's accession to the throne,
Thomas was confirmed as a Knight of the Body and Privy
Councillor. In 1487, he was created Baron Gainsborough.

By the time Thomas II died in 1496, the Old Hall as we know it today was established and was the seat of the Burgh family. The partially surviving inventory for his goods at probate lists Lord Burgh's house as having a hall, a parlour, an inner parlour, a withdrawing room, a great chamber with another chamber next to it, a chamber in the tower, and a chamber in the gallery. Other unknown rooms were probably listed on the missing part of the document.

Lord Thomas is known to have been buried in the parish church of All Saints alongside his wife Margaret (who had died in 1488) and within sight of the Old Hall. Because his son and successor, Edward Burgh, was never summoned to Parliament, it is arguable that the baronetcy bestowed upon Thomas II had also died with him.

Edward Lord Burgh, 1464-1528

At the age of thirteen Edward's marriage to nine-year-old widow, Anne Cobham, had been arranged by his father Thomas II. Anne was the daughter of Sir Thomas 5th Baron Cobham of Starborough. (Anne's first husband, Edward Blount, had died aged eight years old).

Sir Thomas II is known to have obtained a papal dispensation in 1477 for the couple to marry because they were, albeit distantly, related to each other. Thomas II had probably been keen on this union in order to bring some further 'blue blood' into the parvenu Burgh family line. (It was also by this marriage that Starborough Castle came into the ownership of the Burgh family).

Initially at least, Edward endeavoured to follow in his father's illustrious example. He won a knighthood on the battlefield of Stoke in 1487, was the Member of Parliament for Lincoln in 1492 and in November 1494 he distinguished himself in a tournament at Westminster.

However, unlike his late father's successful dealings with a succession of monarchs, Edward Burgh's own relationship with his King went quickly and terribly awry. We do not know the precise reason but it may have been due to his association with others that the monarch distrusted. This was a time of great concern for Henry Tudor with plots against him to contend with, treason and pretenders to the throne. It may also have marked the onset of Edward's mental illness.

On 18th December 1496, Edward was forced to bind himself to Henry VII in a legal bond promising that he would appear before the king whenever summoned and made to vow to do his subjects no harm. Moreover, Edward had to remain in the custody of King Henry's Lord Chamberlain unless given royal permission to leave. If he broke those conditions, Edward would then owe the king the huge sum of 5,000 marks. Unsurprisingly Edward Burgh was not summoned to take up his father's seat in Parliament in the January of 1497.

After being made to make two further such promises, by May 1497 Edward Burgh appears to have been allowed home to Lincolnshire. However not long after he was again the subject of the king's displeasure and incarcerated in the notorious Fleet Prison in London. He was placed under a huge financial guarantee that he would not to try to escape – yet recklessly Edward did escape – putting himself immediately in debt with the king to the sum of thousands of more pounds.

Over the ensuing years, the king's lawyers pursued Sir Edward through the Court of Chancery for ever increasing amounts of money. Then when King Henry VII died in 1509, Edward Burgh was found to be 'distracted of memorie' and declared a lunatic. (This fate also befell Edward's brother-in-law Sir George Tailboys and Lord Ros of Hamlake, all of whom had shared Ros ancestry).

Lady Anne Burgh died 26th June 1526. Although Sir Edward lived until 1528, it appears that he never fully regained normal mental capacity although he did enjoy some lucid periods. On Edward's death his estates passed to his eldest son, Thomas III.

Thomas Burgh III, 1st Baron Burgh of Gainsborough, c.1488-1550

Before his death, Thomas Burgh II had arranged a good marriage for his grandson and namesake, Thomas III, to Agnes the daughter of Sir William Tyrwhitt. It took place in 1496 when young Thomas III was just eight-years old. Through this marriage, Thomas was later able to make useful contacts in Yorkshire and Lincolnshire in his desperate struggle to maintain the Burghs' standing during his father's long mental illness.

Whilst still living Edward Burgh had slid ever further from royal grace, his son Thomas III appears to have fought hard to remain in them. Furthermore, Thomas valiantly tried to restore the family's dwindling fortune. While his father resided at Gainsborough Old Hall, Thomas appears to have lived at Stow Hall (just as his younger brother would do in the future once Thomas in turn had inherited and moved into the Old Hall).

In 1500, Thomas took over his father's position as a justice of the peace in Lindsey and continued his service in local government into the reign of the incoming King – which was as much as could be expected of him as a local leading figure who was awaiting his father's eventual demise before coming into his own.

Thomas combined his local duties alongside a career at court and, just like his grandfather and father before him, with military service. Eventually in 1513, having been one of the King's Spears (or bodyguard of Henry VIII) Thomas was knighted on Flodden Field after victory over the Scots.

Although Thomas III was Sheriff of Lincoln in 1518-19 and again in 1524-25, over the ensuing years he would never quite match up to his Grandfather's meteoric rise. The dark stain of his father's disastrous life, no doubt coupled with the terrible stigma attached to his madness, may have overshadowed Thomas's efforts. He did however manage to bring a welcome degree of stability to the Burgh family which undoubtedly helped salvage their long term prospects. Thomas Burgh III's safe and dependable approach led to him being created 'Lord Borough de Gaynesboro' in 1529 and heralded the return of the Burgh family to the House of Lords. (Sixteenth century records treated his baronetcy as a new creation. However in 1916 when the Burgh peerage was drawn out of abeyance, it was given precedence as of 1487, which has caused some confusion when assessing whether there were in fact four or five 'Lord Burghs').

Unlike his illustrious grandfather, Thomas III does not appear to have become very close to his monarch – even though while at court he must have regularly come into close contact with Henry VIII.

Having been appointed as Anne Boleyn's Lord Chamberlain, in May 1533 Thomas III maintained a high profile, even riding in the queen's barge on her coronation day as she was received at the Tower of London. During the ensuing procession, Burgh had the honour of holding the middle of the queen's coronation train.

In April 1534, Lord Burgh was mistakenly reported to have died (Letters and Papers, Foreign and Domestic, Henry VIII, Volume 8). The letter read 'Lord Borow and Mr. Baynton, the Queen's chamberlains, are dead." In fact Lord Burgh was alive but tragically had lost his eldest son, Edward, shortly before. Edward had briefly been married to Catherine Parr, future wife of King Henry VIII. It is not known if Catherine ever fell pregnant by Edward Burgh, certainly no child is recorded as having lived to full term or survived infancy. It was also rumoured that Edward had showed signs of madness.

Catherine Parr

In May 1536, Thomas III found himself in the dreadful position of being chosen as one of twenty-six peers – summoned to the trial of Anne Boleyn, an event that must have caused him a degree of personal regret and anxiety.

See 'Faith and the Old Hall'

Sometime not long after this, Thomas III and Agnes Burgh's second eldest son Thomas died. This must have been yet another terrible blow for Lord Burgh, and an especially unhappy time for all concerned when in 1543, Lord Thomas obtained a private Act of Parliament in order to bastardise the children of his deceased son's wife, Elizabeth Owen, on the grounds of her adultery during her husband's lifetime.

At about this time Lady Agnes Burgh died. Thomas III then married middle-aged, twice widowed Alice Beddingfield, the daughter of William London. It may be that by this time Gainsborough Old Hall had fallen out of favour with Thomas Burgh. It appears that he chose to live out his final days with Lady Alice 'my welbeloved wyf' 'elsewhere – probably at the Rokewood family seat (left to Alice by her first husband Edmund Rokewood) of Euston Hall in the backwaters of Suffolk.

In Burgh's will (written and dated at London on 28th February 1550) he describes himself as *'Sir Thomas Burgh Knight, Lord Burgh of Ewston in the Countie of Suffolk'* and not of Gainsborough Old Hall which no longer appears even worthy of mention by name among his various other properties in such far flung places as London and Calais. Lord Burgh also seems to have regretted his bastardisation of at least one of his 'grandchildren', for in that will he leaves money for not only his daughter Dorothy's wedding but also
'700 marks towards the preferment and marriage of Margaret, daughter of Dame Elizabeth Burgh, late wife to Sir Thomas my son deceased…
Then he instructs his executors to *'sell so moche of my woodes in Gaynesburgh… as shall amownte to the said full some…'*

William Lord Burgh, 1522-1584

William was Thomas Burgh III's eldest surviving son and heir and was married to Katherine Fynes, the daughter of Lord Clinton, Earl of Lincoln. Before her marriages, in 1519 Katherine's mother, as the young Elizabeth 'Bessie' Blount, had given birth to Henry Fitzroy, Duke of Richmond – the only illegitimate son of King Henry VIII to be recognised. She was married shortly after her son's birth to Sir Gilbert Tailboys, and then on his death to Edward Lord Clinton (then Lord Admiral of England).

William took his seat in Parliament on 26th January 1552 and continued to be summoned until January 1581. He owned properties in Kent, Northumberland, Suffolk, Surrey and London.

As 'William Borow' he was admitted into Gray's Inn in 1569 and in 1573 was one of the Peers at the trial of the Duke of Norfolk. Two years later, in a letter to the Earl of Richmond, William states that he has admitted his own son Henry into the fellowship of Lincolns Inn. Sadly just two years later in January 1578, Henry was killed during a duel. William's youngest son, John, is believed to have died in a duel in 1594.

William almost certainly resided much, if not all of the time, at Sterborough Castle, near Lingfield in Surrey, conveniently placed for business in London, and by the time of his death at Lambeth in October 1584, Gainsborough was little used as a major residence.

Thomas Burgh IV, c.1558-1597

One of William's younger sons, Thomas, succeeded his father and took his seat in the House of Lords in 1584. (Many publications describe him as '5th Lord and Baron Gainsborough', although perhaps technically he ought not to be referred to as such).

According to 'Parishes: Chidingstone', The History and Topological Survey of the County of Kent Vol. 3 -1797', *'Thomas, lord Burgh, resided, as his ancestors had done, at Sterborough-castle, and was a man of no small eminence…'*

Two years later, Thomas IV was appointed Governor of the Brill in the Netherlands as a part of the English contribution to the Dutch revolt against Spain. He was made a Knight of the Garter for his services. However, it would appear from his letters home that the Brill did much to weaken Burgh in both health and spirit.

During his long absences from England, his personal finances began to fall to pieces, making Lord Thomas more worthy of the title 'Lord Borrow' than Burgh.

Meanwhile at his Gainsborough estate Burgh's tenants began to do as they pleased in his absence. In 1587 the Privy Council had to issue a letter to William Towers ordering him to desist from disturbing Lord Burgh's lands there and not to molest his bailiff. In May of that same year another letter from the Privy Council was sent to the Sheriff of Lincoln telling him to hold his hand over debts incurred by Burgh until his return from the Netherlands. The following year yet another letter from them instructs the Sheriff to leave the Burgh lands alone. Without Lord Thomas to oversee his estates they floundered and he became deeply in debt to two leading London moneylenders.

By 1595, fearing for both her husband's sinking health and wealth, Lady Frances Burgh begged Queen Elizabeth for her husband's return. Sir Robert Sydney commented in November 1595: *'God send (another lady) better success than my Lady Borow, whose desire was absolutely denied and the Queen took it very ill that in such time he could desire to be from this government.'*

In 1596 an almost bankrupt Thomas Burgh was forced to sell the Gainsborough Old Estate. William Hickman purchased it.

The following year, Lord Burgh was suggested as Deputy of Ireland – an unpopular posting – and sent there early in 1597. That year he died at Newry of typhus on October 14th aged just 39. His body was returned home and buried at Westminster. In his will, Thomas expresses the hope that Her Majesty will receive his wife and children into her protection, he having spent his patrimony, and ended his days, in her service.

However Lady Burgh and her three young children were left in penury. In February 1598 Lord Sydney received a letter stating that: 'Lady Borow is in great poverty… Eventually Queen Elizabeth dealt with the situation by letting it be known that she wished that whoever was then appointed to the now vacant post of Governor of Brill might give £500 a year to Lady Frances for her maintenance.

Lord and Lady Burgh's only son, Robert, was just three years old when his father died. He passed away whilst in the care of the Bishop of Winchester on February 26th, 1602. Robert was buried as 'Lord Burroughs' in Winchester Cathedral. With no heir, the title became extinct and so this dynasty of Burghs and their long association with Gainsborough came to an abrupt end.

Lady Frances lived on for some fifty years or so after her husband's death and was buried at St Margaret's, Westminster in July 1647.

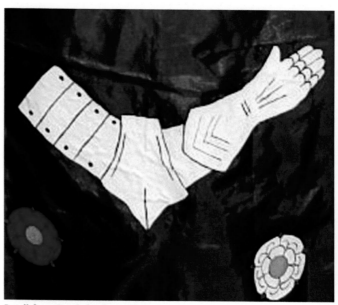

Detail from Burgh family emblem

The Origins of the Hickman Family

The ancestor of this particular Hickman family line is said to have come to England with William the Conqueror. However the earliest recorded member of the family is Richard Hickman, Lord of the manors of Bloxham and Wickham, in Oxfordshire in 1272. Richard was a man of some consideration as his eldest son John served in Parliament as one of the knights of the county of Oxfordshire.

After John's death, the estate passed to brother William, whose oldest son Roger served as a 'much esteemed and valiant commander' in France with King Edward III. The estate then passed on down the Hickman line until 1409 when William Hickman is mentioned as lord of the manor of Woodford-Hall in Essex, which remained as the family residence until 1539, when Walter Hickman inherited the estate on the death of his brother, William.

As the younger son and therefore not having expected to inherit, Walter had already made his way in the world as a successful merchant in London. When Walter died in October 1540, the estates then passed to his younger son, Anthony Hickman, also by this time a very successful and rich Mercer in London and a favourite of King Henry VIII. Anthony was by this time in partnership with fellow mercer and merchant-adventurer, Thomas Locke, the son of the King's Royal Mercer, Sir William Locke.

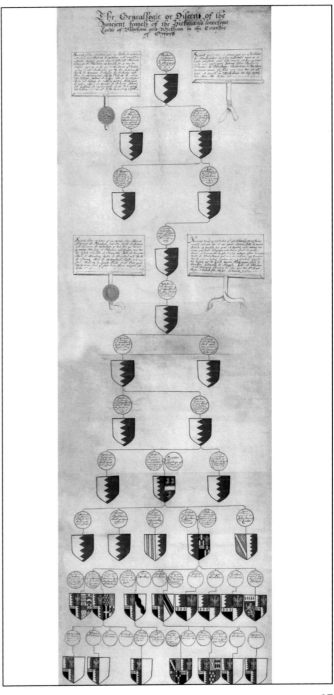

Unlike Lord Thomas Burgh III (his contemporary at court), Sir William Locke had been close to King Henry VIII. Not only was he the king's Royal Mercer (and in this capacity probably had accompanied King Henry VIII on his visit to Gainsborough Old Hall in 1541) but he was also trusted enough to have a key to the King's bedroom and to be 'vouchsafed' for His Majesty to dine at the Locke's London home. He also acted as a spy for Henry whilst on trips overseas.

Rose Locke-Hickman, 1526-1613

In partnership with her brother Thomas Locke, Rose's husband Anthony Hickman is known to have owned many ships, including one named 'Mary Rose' (which was later used in 1596 on a raid on Cadiz, Spain). After Thomas' death, Anthony Hickman is also known to have owned amongst others 'The Great Christopher' (given to Queen Elizabeth I's navy in 1560 and renamed 'Victory'). Anthony and Rose married in 1543.

Anthony and Rose Hickman had at least nine children, only seven of whom lived into adulthood. By this time Anthony had broken ties with Woodford Hall and owned a number of properties around Cheapside in London, where the family lived, as well as 'two faire houses, the one in London and the other in Rumforde, Essex' and a 'fair house in Antwerpe' which he rented during exile for £70 a year. Anthony died in 1573.

Rose then married widower Simon Throckmorton of Brampton (d 1585). However, nowhere does this name appear on her portrait of 1596 (although she identifies herself as 'Rose Throckmorton' in writings she made at Gainsborough in 1610 at the age of 84). The Throckmorton name had become scandalized late in Queen Elizabeth I's reign and so perhaps the Hickman family chose to distance themselves from it.

The Hickman's first child was daughter, Mary, (b.1547). By her second husband, merchant Richard Phillips of Middlesex, she had a son, Jerome, who later became the vicar at All Saints parish church at Gainsborough from 1604 until his resignation in April 1608 – the time of the Separatists' escape to Holland.

ÆTATIS 70. 1596. XBRIS. 2 7.

Rose Daugh.ᵗ to Sᵗ Wᵐ Lock Kᵗ married to Anthony Hickman.

?-1625
ghby)

Hickman's eldest son, William
e his father, he became a successful
as being a Justice of the Peace in
iam purchased Gainsborough Old
h his first wife, Agnes (widow of Sir
or of London). After Agnes' death in
izabeth Willoughby by whom he

William Hickman, 1549-1625   **Lady Elizabeth (Willoughby)**

distinguished career at Cambridge University, second
son, Henry (1550- 1618) became a Doctor of Law and a civil
lawyer. He was Chancellor for the Diocese of Peterborough
(1587), J.P.Q. Northamptonshire (by 1592), and Member of
Parliament for Northampton.

On June 16th 1549 the Hickman's eldest son, William Hickman,
was born. Like his father, he became a successful merchant
and is named as being a Justice of the Peace in the Middlesex
rolls. William purchased Gainsborough Old Hall in 1596,
arriving with his first wife, Agnes (widow of Sir Wolstan Dixie,
Lord Mayor of London). After Agnes' death in 1600, William
married Elizabeth Willoughby by whom he had all his children.

After a distinguished career at Cambridge University, second
son, Henry (1550- 1618) became a Doctor of Law and a civil
lawyer. He was Chancellor for the Diocese of Peterborough
(1587), J.P.Q. Northamptonshire (by 1592), and Member of
Parliament for Northampton.

Walter Hickman, 1553-1617   **Anthony Hickman, 1560-1597**

Walter Hickman, 1553-1617
Anthony Hickman, 1560-1597

Third son Walter, (1552-1617) was entrenched in the
London world of business and with life-long interests at
court- including a position as Gentleman Usher to Queen
Elizabeth I. He is also listed as a Justice of the Peace in the
Middlesex rolls and in 1613 was returned as Member of
Parliament for Mitchell.

Around 1554, during the reign of Bloody Queen Mary, Rose
gave birth to an unknown child at *'Chilswell'* near Oxford
before joining her husband, Anthony, in exile in Antwerp.

This child presumably died in infancy. Another male child
was born in Antwerp, but he also seems to have died young.

Son Anthony, (1560-1597) was born on the family's return
to London from exile. Anthony was at Peterhouse,
Cambridge at the same time as Robert 'Troublechurch'
Brown (the founder of the Separatist or 'Brownists'
movement) and senior to a very young William Brewster.
In 1583 he moved to Corpus Christi where he became the
subject of a long dispute, the heart of the matter being that
he had somehow procured a dispensation, signed by Queen
Elizabeth herself, 'excusing' him from taking orders before
receiving his Fellowship, leading to strong speculation that
he was also of Separatist leanings.

Although this original dispute was settled in his favour, Anthony found himself again under attack by new master, John Jegon and left Cambridge in 1592/93. As a Doctor of the Civil Law, he practiced in London. He died unmarried aged 37. In his will Anthony left his seal ring, which bore his name and was always kept tied on his purse string, to his mother Rose.

The date on Anthony's portrait has been over-painted '1603' in error and should read 1596.

Son Eleazar (1562-1618) was named after John Knox's son. Little is known about his life other than that he was 'Gentleman Usher to Ludovic Stuart, Duke of Lennox and Richmond' and that he died unmarried and without issue.

The last of the Hickman sons was Matthew (c.1563). Little is known about him other than in a family document dating from 1637 where he is described as 'clerk' and that he had 'dyed since his mother…' The same names his three daughters, Frances, Mary and Rose.

The Gainsborough Hickmans

Willoughby Hickman, 1604-1649
Lady Bridget (Thornaugh), 1606-1683

Willoughby was the first true Gainsborough Hickman both to own the Old Hall and to be baptized in the town. He had the unenviable position of being Lord of the Manor during the English Civil War but managed to weather the storm relatively intact. Having originally intended to remain neutral, Willoughby was created a baronet by King Charles I and then subsequently fined by the Parliamentarians for his 'delinquency', but the fine was subsequently reduced. There are no known portraits of either.

William Hickman, 1628-1682
Lady Elizabeth (Neville), 1635-

Sir William was Sheriff of Nottinghamshire in 1653/4 among numerous other positions he held. From 1660 until his death, he was MP for Retford. A cast iron fire back now in the east range bears the date 1658 and the Hickman family arms marking the high point of William's career.

William Hickman 1628- 1682

Lady Elizabeth (Neville) 1635 -

Willoughby Hickman, 1659-1720

Lady Ann (Anderson), 1666-

Neville Hickman, 1701-1733

Lady Frances Hall, c.1700

Willoughby Hickman, 1659-1720
Lady Ann (Anderson), 1666-

William's eldest surviving son Willoughby, succeeded his father. Older brothers, William and Francis, had already died. Like his father, Willoughby pursued a career in Parliament becoming MP for Kingston upon Hull in 1685, Retford in 1698 and Lincolnshire from 1713 until his death.

Neville Hickman, 1701-1733
Lady Frances Hall, c.1700

By the time that Neville Hickman inherited Gainsborough Old Hall it was woefully unfashionable and beyond renovation and remodeling for it to live up to the expectation of the Georgian style of life. Before his death Neville had built the new Hickman family residence just a few miles away at Thonock. It was then that the manor house at Gainsborough became known as 'The Old Hall' and although the family no longer lived there it remained in their ownership.

Neville George Hickman, 1725-1781
Lady Frances Elizabeth (Tower), b.1722

Sir Neville George succeeded his father while still a minor. He had three daughters, Frances, Rose-Elizabeth and Ann who died in infancy. Elizabeth married and had two sons who died young leaving Frances as the heir to the Hickman estate.

Lady Frances Elizabeth (Tower), b.1722

Lady Frances Hickman, 1747-1826

Frances was a charitable person, giving a part of the Old Hall gardens in 1794 to be used by the parish as an extension to the by then overcrowded grave yard. She also gave land for a school for poor girls and boys. Lay Frances did not have any children and so after two hundred and thirty years in the ownership of the Hickman family, Gainsborough Old Hall passed into that of the Bacons.

Henry Bacon Hickman, 1788-1862

On Lady Frances' death, the ownership of the Old Hall was willed to her cousin Henry Bacon, on condition that the Hickman family name lived on through him. Thus he became Henry Bacon Hickman bringing about the changes between the two family coats of arms that can be seen today above the internal doors of the Great Hall.

Sir Henry Hickman Bacon, 1820-1872
Lady Elizabeth (Beckett), 1829-1885

When Henry Hickman Bacon died unmarried, he left the Old Hall to his nephew, who became Sir Henry Hickman-Bacon Bart.

Sir Henry Hickman Bacon, 1820-1872

Lady Elizabeth (Beckett), 1829-1885

Sir Hickman Beckett Bacon 1855-1945

Henry and Elizabeth's son Hickman Beckett Bacon, although residing at the family home at Thonock, carried out repairs and alterations to the Old Hall, as the inscription 'HHB 1878' carved below a Victorian gothic-style window above the exterior of the buttery testifies.

Affectionately remembered by many in Lincolnshire as 'Uncle Hicky', life-long bachelor Sir Hickman was considered wonderfully eccentric in his later years.

He was a founder member of the Lincolnshire Automobile Club and became its President in 1902, a position he held until his death 13th April 1945, the eve of his 90th birthday.

Sir Edmund Castell Bacon, 1903-1982

After the death of Hickman Beckett Bacon his nephew Sir Edmund Bacon inherited the Old Hall. It was Sir Edmund who encouraged a group of local people, led by Harold Witty Brace, to form themselves into the Friends of the Old Hall Association with the aim of saving the by then disintegrating manor house from collapse and to turn it into a museum. Without that gallant band of dedicated, forward-thinking people who raised the funds to make urgent repairs, the Old Hall is unlikely to have survived. In 1971 Sir Edmund gave the Old Hall to the nation, and thus followed a major programme of repairs leaving the Old Hall almost as we see it today.

Sir Nicholas Hickman Ponsonby Bacon, (born1953)

Maintains a keen and active interest in the Old Hall and is currently the President of the Friends of the Old Hall Association.

NORTH VIEW OF THE OLD HALL, GAINSBURGH.

Old Hall circa 1817

The Purchase of Gainsborough Old Hall

Gainsborough manor and its estate were sold in 1596 to pay off a London moneylender thus ending the Burgh family's long association with Lincolnshire. London- based William Hickman purchased it for a reputed five-thousand-two-hundred pounds (between five and six million pounds at today's value).

William's seventy-year-old, twice-widowed mother, Lady Rose, also came to live at Gainsborough Old Hall and is buried in the church.

By this time, the Gainsborough estate had suffered an absentee Lord of the manor for decades. Thomas Burgh IV's bailiffs are known to have been molested by local people who were owed money. As a result Burgh's tenants began to do as they wished.

It appears that Gainsborough had become somewhat of a 'closed town' as far as trade went. Outside traders were only encouraged into town for the twice-yearly markets (held in the Mart yard). In short, it made for the perfect condition for a price-fixing cartel to become established by the local landowners and suppliers of food. This would have resulted in artificially high prices, which in turn would have especially affected the poor.

It was a situation that would pose the incoming William Hickman many problems and when he tried to remedy the situation it made him very unpopular with some. With local Lincolnshire traders no doubt unwilling to evoke the wrath of the Gainsborough worthies, Hickman invited London traders into town in a bid to break the local cartel. He also sought to extend the twice-yearly markets.

John Thorold, a local aristocrat, became particular opposed to Sir William, describing him disdainfully as 'a threadbare fellow'. Considering Hickman's great wealth this may seem strange, but as a godly man and devout Puritan, William would not have believed in making a great outward show of this wealth by perpetually adorning himself with expensive new clothes in order to impress others. A flurry of court actions against Hickman by disenchanted local gentry soon ensued. These until recent times have been used to portray Hickman as the sole 'villain of the piece' and perpetrator of unrest.

Strong opposition had especially rallied when Hickman attempted to collect his rightful revenue from the town's market and a toll from grain ships passing through the port at Gainsborough and the Gainsborough section of the River Trent over which he had legally enforceable riparian rights. In what seems to be reprisal, one of William Hickman's servants was stabbed to death. Recently released letters from the *'Cecil's Papers'* of Hatfield House show William Hickman in an entirely different light than that previously painted in past publications and now bring a sense of balance to the situation so that the reader might draw their own conclusion.

An official précis of a letter addressed to Sir Robert Cecil reads; *'On behalf of Mr. Hickman, in a cause depending before the Council, prosecuted by the malice of Mr. Topliff and other gentlemen of Lincolnshire, who, to stop Hickman's proceedings in the prosecuting of justice against some persons that killed a servant of his, follow this cause among other hard measures. Hickman is both honest and very beneficial to the poor inhabitants of Gainsborough, where he lives. – Hanworth, 8 July 1598'.*

'Mr. Topliff' was the husband of Thomas Burgh III's daughter, Margaret.

Another letter in the Cecil Papers states: *'From William Hickman to unknown (1598.) He (Hickman) purchased the manor of Gainsborough, Lincoln, with toll corn of the market there. Murder of his servant, Martin Furser, by three of Sir George St. Poole's men. In consequence of his prosecuting the offenders, he has been oppressed by St. Poole, Sir William Wray his brother, and Nicholas Girlington and others, who seek to defeat him of the said toll. (Describes their proceedings). Prays his addressee to call the above named before him to answer their misdemeanors, and also to take order for the commitment of the murderers.'*

Far from *'manipulating his authority as Justice of the Peace (at Gainsborough) to prosecute others'* as accused, Hickman is known to have served for many years in Middlesex as a JP without any such complaint. George St. Poole and William Wray were closely related, with Wray having been an MP, and so they might equally be accused of using that connection to try to manipulate the situation. It is also interesting to note that many of the men named in similar actions against William Hickman were related by marriage to the outgoing Burgh family and therefore perhaps unhappy to have then lost any past financial *'advantage's'* enjoyed at Gainsborough on the sale of the estate.

William Hickman was also hated for having 'demolished stalls erected in front of shops in the market place' – a practice of encroachment that was already outlawed in London and other places in order to provide safe passage for pedestrians and traffic along narrow medieval streets.

In 1609 Hickman was vilified for encouraging an influx of poor people on to the town's common land to build shacks, where upon they became an immediate charge on the town's poor rate. (Under the 1601 Elizabethan Poor Law, the poor rate was a tax on a property levied on the parish which was then used to provide poor relief to the poor resident in that parish).

At that time poor people without a fixed abode were considered little more than vagrants and not eligible for any financial support at all. (This raises the question as to where and under what dire conditions these poor folk were living beforehand).

More poor people living within Gainsborough meant that the rich townspeople had to pay more tax to help support them – especially Sir William!

Another complaint arose over William Hickman's refusal to repair the local church. Since Thomas III had moved away and Lord William Burgh had made Sterborough Castle, near Lingfield in Surrey, the prime family residence more than thirty years previously, major members of the Burgh were no longer buried within the parish church of All Saints in Gainsborough. Thomas II left generous amounts in his will to his chantry chapel set up within the main church in return for certain Catholic rituals to be regularly performed in his memory. However, these rituals – along with the chantries themselves – were outlawed after Henry's break with Rome. In short, the church had lost its major benefactor.

By the time William Hickman arrived, All Saints church was evidently suffering neglect and in need of major repairs which the rich local gentry then expected him alone to pay for. Couple this with the fact that Hickman was a staunch Puritan and under no legal obligation to repair any part that was considered as a dissolved chantry (usually an annex to the main building) one can begin to understand his reluctance to do so. Hickman did however have a part in danger of collapse pulled down. As the rest of the church is known to have continued in use for more than a century, this supports the idea that a side chapel was demolished.

This unsettled period in the Hickmans' relationship with Gainsborough did not completely disappear until William Hickman's death, along with those of many of his original ill-wishers.

Faith and The Old Hall

Detail from painting by Edward Board depicting King Edward IV listening to Latimer preach at St Paul's in 1547. Behind the King and wearing the chain of office of Sheriff of London stands Sir William Locke.

Faith and the Old Hall

Whether under the ownership of the Burghs or the Hickmans, across the centuries the Old Hall seems to have been no stranger to sheltering religious dissenters beneath its roof.

Early during the English Reformation under King Henry VIII, instead of paying 'lip service' to the King's break with Rome as many others undoubtedly had, Lord Thomas Burgh III appears to have been a keen convert to the new Protestant faith.

Whilst having declared himself as the head of the now Protestant Church in England, nonetheless King Henry still considered the more radical Lutheran (and newly emerging Calvinist) – style Protestantism to be heresy and punishable by death.

This is intriguing because at that very same time, Anne Boleyn is known to have been privately encouraging this very form of Protestantism. Indeed one of Anne Boleyn's chaplains claimed that Lord Thomas Burgh III often took a lead part in the lively discussions upon the scriptures that are known to have taken place in the queen's household at meal times.

As a part of the queen's inner circle, Lord Burgh must surely have also known William Locke well. Locke too was close enough to Anne Boleyn for his daughter, Lady Rose Hickman, to have written about him as having smuggled in 'heretic' Protestant writings from abroad at that very same time for Boleyn.

Lord Burgh also seems to have been impressed by a radical preacher named Thomas Rose (see Foxe's Book of Martyrs) who at one point preached at Gainsborough regularly, perhaps even in the Burgh's private chapel which was licensed in 1529. Burgh wrote in a letter to Thomas Cromwell that he reckoned Rose was worth as much as at least forty incompetent Lincolnshire clergymen.

Henry VIII

The incoming Hickman family was no stranger to religious conflict, and known to be among active early Evangelical Protestants during the still Catholic phase of King Henry VIII's reign.

Lady Rose Hickman's father, Sir William Locke, was often away at Antwerp in his earlier years at the same time as William Tyndale was active there and it was probably his English language version of the Bible that he smuggled into England. In her writing of 1610, Lady Rose also recalls reading from these:

> *'My mother in the dayes of King Henry the 8th came to some light of the gospel by meanes of some English books sent privately to her by my fathers factor from beyond the sea: where upon she used to call me with my 2 sisters into her chamber to read to us out of these same good books very privately for feare of troble because these good books were then accepted hereticall...'*

Rose's mother had good reason to be fearful. Another known Bible smuggler, Robert Packington, was shot dead close to the Locke home in Cheapside in London. A member of the clergy later admitted on his deathbed to having been a party to Packington's assassination.

Both Rose's husband, Anthony Hickman, and her eldest brother, Thomas Locke, appear to have been 'favourites' of King Henry VIII and his son King Edward VI. Although both grew extremely rich through their 'adventures, they had according to Rose;

> *'learned not to trust in uncertaine riches but in the Living Lord who giveth abundantly all things to be enjoyed :for they were not unmindfull to use and imploy their substance to the glory of God and good of his church, as they daily manifested by giving entertainment to Byshop Hooper, Mr Foxe, Mr Knoxe and his other godly preaches of which some afterward did suffer martordom in Queene Maryes dayes, who if they were living on earth, as undoubtedly they are in heaven would not forget...'*

Lady Rose Hickman

Rose tells how, early during the reign of Queen Mary, her family and friends had defied the monarch by continuing to hold clandestine religious services in their own home, but always, as she explained, with one eye cast firmly upon the door.

She also tells of how at that time, her husband and brother had helped to spirit wanted Protestants from out of the country. Among those were probably some of those she named previously (John Knox in particular is known to have been a close friend of both the Lockes and Anthony Hickman. Rose's sister-in-law, Anne Vaughn-Locke went into exile to Geneva with him. Knox often mentions the Hickmans in his later letters). As well as helping these Protestants to escape, Rose says they provided them with financial support.

Eventually Anthony and Thomas were arrested. They were sent to the notorious Fleet Prison and tortured but refused to admit to anything. Eventually, after release from the Fleet and under house arrest, Anthony escaped to Antwerp. Subsequently Rose was forced to flee England too and to go into exile abroad with her husband and family until Mary had died. Broken by his experiences in the prison, and under pressure from his wife to remain in England, Thomas Locke chose to remain in England and to pretend to conform to the Catholic faith. He died within the year.

However, once having returned to England on the accession of Queen Elizabeth I, the Hickmans still found themselves at odds with the official Church of England. The Anglican Church, as settled by Queen Elizabeth, was described by John Knox as 'bastard' and a 'stinking pile of old works' which the Hickmans should have nothing to do with. Thus, the family became known by the derogatory term *'Puritan'*. This was coined to describe those, who like them, hankered after the purer church as settled in the time of King Edward VI and for the true completion of the English Reformation.

According to documents in the *Portland Papers*, Lady Rose Hickman's third son, Anthony, was involved in a long dispute at Corpus Christi, Cambridge centering upon his own Puritan stance. Prior to his taking up his fellowship at Corpus Christi, Anthony had been at Peterhouse and was a contemporary of Robert 'Troublechurch' Browne (considered founder of the 'Brownists' Or 'Separatist' movement), John Greenwood and a very young William Brewster (who would later be known as Elder Brewster of Pilgrim Fathers in the New World). In fact there is circumstantial evidence to show that Anthony may have indeed been of the Separatist persuasion himself. After leaving Cambridge around 1592, Anthony settled in London close to the known Separatist congregation there before dying in 1597.

In an attempt to curb the aspirations of such 'dissidents' and having executed Separatists John Greenwood and Henry Barrowe in April 1593, within weeks Queen Elizabeth's government brought about the 'Act Against Puritans', whereby it became illegal to be a Puritan or to encourage others to become likewise. Subsequent persecution of Puritans would not be confined to matters of faith. Life for those seeking official appointments at court suddenly became more difficult. Walter Hickman, already deeply entrenched within court circles, had often brokered many such appointments in the past and in the usual Elizabethan way- by offering financial inducements to those in power.

With the wars with Spain taking a toll on English merchants such as William Hickman, such an appointment with its consequent income would have proved very useful at such a difficult time. However, it is clear from letters in the Cecil Paper that when Walter applied in 1594 for, and expected to obtain, the position of Receiver of the Court of Wards on behalf of his brother William, it was refused – even though the sum of £1,000 (equivalent to almost a million pounds today) had been offered in return.

It is this growing situation of hostility towards Puritans in London that may have precipitated William Hickman's move to Lincolnshire and the purchase of Gainsborough Old Hall.

Another consideration would have been the possibility of increased religious persecution and the question of succession once the aging Queen Elizabeth died, bringing with it a threat of an enforced return for England to Catholicism. In either case, having access and control over one's own ships in one's own private port would have proved a very attractive prospect.

Although there is no one defining document proving that the Hickman family gave shelter to the Separatist congregation of John Smyth at Gainsborough (some of whom went on to become known as Pilgrim Fathers) the foregoing circumstantial evidence to support this theory is very strong.

Lady Rose Hickman, by then in her eighties, was still very much alive and living at the Old Hall. Added to this, it would seem implausible that the vicar of the nearby parish church would not have known about such a congregation on his 'door step' and reported them to the church authorities. The vicar in question of all Saints' from 1602 until his resignation in April 1608 was Jerome Phillipps, a known radical Puritan minister and the son of Lady Rose Hickman's late daughter Mary. Phillipps had studied alongside Separatist John Robinson at Corpus Christi, Cambridge.

Yet despite this evidence, there is a minority who refute that William Hickman might have supported John Smyth's Separatist congregation in the town. They cite instead William Hickman's reporting of Gainsborough man, John Noble, to the authorities for *'non-conformity'*.(Noble had not taken Holy Communion for twelve months – a sacrament vigorously upheld by Puritans, Separatists and Anglicans alike. Also, Noble had rudely refused to remove his hat in church in the presence of his Lord of the Manor, William Hickman).

Interestingly, a member of John Smyth's Gainsborough Separatist congregation was Thomas Helwys who, although having initially escaped to Holland with Smyth and the others, later returned to London to form the first known Baptist church there.

Lady Rose Hickman's fourth great-grandson, Sir Neville Gorge Hickman seems to have carried on the family's association with those of non-conformist belief. On Friday 3rd August 1759, the then considered 'dissident' John Wesley wrote: *'I preached in Gainsborough, in Sir Nevil Hickman's great hall… I was walking back through a gaping, staring crowd, when Sir Nevil came and thanked me for my sermon, to the no small amazement of his neighbours, who shrank back as if they had seen a ghost.'*

Over the coming years, Wesley would return to preach inside the Great Hall several times more.

At 84 years of age Wesley wrote: *'In the evening I preached to a large congregation in Sir Nevil Hickman's yard: but Sir Nevil is no more, and has left no son; so the very name of this ancient family is lost! And how changed is that house since I was young, and the good Sir Willoughby Hickman lived here…'*

John Wesley

Richard III in the Great Hall (re-enactors)

....

....

....

....

....

....

....

....

....

....

Great Hall serving wench (re-enactor)

ALSO BY SUE ALLEN:

The Mayflower Maid

The first part of the New World Trilogy

400 years ago a group of like minded men and women fled England and religious persecution to start a new life on a new continent – America.

One woman's story begins here....

In the infant colony of Plymouth in 1623 a woman lies consumed with fever. In her delirium she insists her name is not the one everyone has come to know and love her by.

The story of Dorothy's tragic journey amongst the Pilgrim Fathers is a vivid and moving account of a pivotal moment in history. The story of how she became the Mayflower Maid is an unforgettable tale of love and loss set amidst the strife and religious bigotry of Seventeenth Century England.

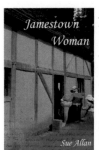

Jamestown Woman

The second part of the New World Trilogy

Having weathered the perils of the Mayflower's voyage and the early days of the Plymouth colony; Dorothy neé Bessie and her husband Thomas are now cast adrift into even more stormy and dangerous waters. Seventeenth century politics are a violent and deadly business, as they are about to find out.

Sue Allen continues her spellbinding chronicles of the Mayflower Maid in 'Jamestown Woman', and once again fate casts her and Thomas into the paths of the great and not so good. The giant firgures of King James I, Captain John Smith and Oliver Cromwell cast their shadows over the lives of the Puritans as England is about to be engulfed by the horrors of The Civil war.

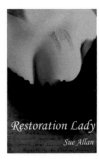

Restoration Lady

The third and final part of New World Trilogy

The much anticipated finale to this wonderful story following events in post civil war England.

Stripped of her title and wealth Bessie faces revenge from past enemies, accusations of witchcraft and the catastrophes of the plague and Great Fire of London.

This concluding part of the New World Trilogy is gripping reading for all followers of Bessie – the Mayflower Maid.

Tudor Rose

The story of the reformation, told through the voice of a woman of the times

Lady Rose Hickman was an extraordinary woman of courage, who lived through one of the most turbulent periods in English History and survived the reigns of two Tudor Kings and nine Tudor queens to tell her remarkable tale...

From her father's Bible smuggling days at the Catholic Court of King Henry VIII, her brothers courageous voyages of exploration, to her final years at Gainsborough Old Hall. Under Queen Elizabeth, Lady Rose and her family suffered persecution as Puritan reformers and gave sanctuary to the Separatists who spawned the Mayflower Pilgrims of America.

Lady Rose Hickman

A complete overview of her life and family

Lady Rose Hickman lived at Gainsborough Old Hall from 1596 until her death in 1613. In 1610, at the age of 84, Rose wrote an account of some of the events in her life, living through the reigns of two Tudor kings and nine Tudor queens and into that of King James Stuart.

In 1543, seventeen-year old Rose married one of King Henry VIII's favourites, Anthony Hickman. The Hickman family originated in Oxford, but Anthony was a London Mercer and merchant adventurer in partnership with Rose's brother, Thomas.

As a result of helping many leading Protestants and their families to escape from persecution, both Anthony and Thomas were imprisoned in the infamous Fleet prison in London. Although eventually released, it was thought prudent for the pair to flee to the Low Countries. Rose's family remained here until the death of Queen Mary and the ascension of Protestant Queen Elizabeth I to the English throne.

Steps along the Mayflower Trail

Steps along the Mayflower Trail is not intended to be a book about the Mayflower Pilgrims – or Separatists, as they were known before their voyage to America.

Instead, this book has been written as a reference companion for those who are already familiar with the Separatists' saga – but who are perhaps not so familiar with the places that feature in it.

'Steps along the Mayflower Trail', sets out to illuminate those villages, towns and buildings in the three counties of Lincolnshire, Yorkshire and Nottinghamshire, that played major roles in their odyssey. These are places that many of the Separatists would have once known as home.

Designed and produced by Domtom Publishing Ltd

Text by Sue Allen

Printed in Great Britain by DPS Partnership Ltd

www.dpsltd.net